HIDDEN

A True Story of the Holocaust

Fanya Gottesfeld Heller

with Joshua M. Greene

SCHOLASTIC INC.

Dedicated to my children,
Miriam, Benjamin, and Jacqueline.

To my dear friend Florence Felig.

And to young people.
May you always live with hope,
dignity, and love.

ISBN 978-1-338-18946-9

10 9 8 7 6 5 4   17 18 19 20 21

Printed in the U.S.A.   40

First printing 2017

Book design by Charice Silverman

CHAPTER ONE

September 26, 1942— No Time to Lose

"THEY'RE COMING!" my aunt Lolla shouted.

I peered out the second-floor window of my maternal grandparents' villa. Through an early-morning haze I saw men in German uniforms jumping off trucks. The Germans were carrying rifles and yelling and kicking in the doors of houses up and down the main street of our town, Skala. Some of the men restrained big barking dogs on leashes. I heard people screaming and watched as men, women, and children scattered in all directions.

For days my family had heard rumors that there would be such an *Aktion,* a roundup of Jews. Sixteen members of my family had gathered in my grandparents' villa, including me, my younger brother, Arthur, my mother and father, and a dozen other family members. We had prepared for this emergency and rehearsed what to do. At the far end of my grandparents' backyard was a warehouse where eggs were packed in boxes for export to Germany. Under the floor of the warehouse my father and uncles had dug a hole where we could hide.

We quickly ran out the back door of my grandparents' villa. The night air was freezing. I wore only my nightgown, without a coat or shoes, but there was no time to change clothes. Everyone ran to the warehouse. We heard gunshots and more people screaming from nearby streets. The Germans were coming closer.

We scrambled silently into the warehouse and climbed down a ladder to the hiding place. My father slid a wooden cover over the hole, and we waited in darkness. Within minutes, boots trampled across the floor over our heads. We were terrified and breathing heavily but nobody dared to make a sound. Then a voice from above our heads called out in German, "Bring the dogs!" There was barking and sniffing. The smell of broken eggs must have covered our scent, because the dogs did not find us.

"No Jews here!" one of the Germans yelled. Again there were footsteps, then silence. None of us moved or shuffled our feet, in case the Germans were only pretending to be gone. Sweat dripped down my body from the heat of so many people packed so tightly together. No fresh air could enter the cramped hole, and I became dizzy. What would I do, I wondered half deliriously, if the Germans found us, and a soldier stuck his rifle in my face? Would I cry? Would I wet myself? Would I beg him not to shoot me?

Hours later my father slowly pushed aside the wooden cover of our hole and peeked out. It seemed that the Germans were gone, but we couldn't be sure. "Better wait here one more day," my father whispered, and he slid the wooden cover back over the opening. For another day we sat in total silence, urinating in our clothing, with no food or water and barely enough air to breathe.

The day of the action was my eighteenth birthday. In those next two days, I grew up very quickly.

CHAPTER TWO

1930—Rumors

I COME FROM SKALA, a small town in eastern Poland. Skala means "rock," as the old city had been built on a rocky hill. When I was a little girl, there were about 5,500 people in Skala. About 3,000 of them were Greek Orthodox Ukrainians. People of Ukrainian ancestry lived in Skala because national borders had shifted more than once over many years. About 1,000 of our neighbors were Catholic Poles. The remaining 1,500 were Jews.

Many of the non-Jews had little good to say about the Jews. People often fear what they do not understand, and we Jews had a culture that was different from our neighbors. Jews had their own way of worship, their own songs, and their own kinds of food. Jews were considered the "others," different from the "normal" non-Jews.

The priests in Skala told churchgoers that Jews

had killed their Lord, Jesus Christ. Some of our neighbors were determined to make us pay for that in one way or another. Non-Jewish merchants charged Jews more for their goods and services. When the townspeople drank too much, they threw stones at Jews or beat them up. Some Christian kids called us names and yelled at us, "Go to Palestine!" which is what the country known as Israel today was called at the time. Still, despite the anti-Semitism, Jewish grown-ups found ways to live and work side by side with their neighbors.

In Skala, no building was more than four stories tall. There were only a few cars, and people moved about in horse-drawn wagons. Most of the townspeople were working-class folks who included shopkeepers, farmers, carpenters, and shoemakers. The poorer townspeople worked two or more jobs, doing laundry, housecleaning, and other manual labor, and saved money by sewing their children's clothes themselves.

Businesses included a flour mill, a farmers market, a company that produced lubricants for machinery, and warehouses that packaged and exported fresh produce. Along the dusty streets of town, merchants sold fabric, shoes, coats, hats, quilts, and other goods from shops and wooden carts. Thanks to the Zbrucz (zzz-BROOCH) River that ran by the town, the soil around Skala was fertile. Farmers harvested abundant crops of wheat, rye, barley, oats, and other grains. They packaged their goods in big burlap bags, which were then sold and exported to Europe and America. The wealthier people lived just outside town in two- and three-story homes built of brick and surrounded by farmland. Jews were not allowed to own land, and most Jews, including my family, lived in town in one-story wooden houses heated by coal- or wood-burning stoves.

Each day when I came home from school I walked into our house and smelled the fragrance of my mother's home-cooked meals. I can still remember the delicious aromas coming from the kitchen, the mouthwatering scents of grated potatoes, steamy clouds of boiling sugar beets, and pots of chicken stew simmering with carrots and onions on our iron stove. I also remember the scents of wax candles that we lit every Friday evening to mark the beginning of Shabbat. And I remember the fragrance of clothes hand-washed and slowly drying in the backyard on ropes suspended from trees under the warm summer sun. None of our homes had electricity or running water.

The town of Skala was not much to look at, but if you left the main street and ventured into the countryside, you found dense forests and broad fields. When we weren't in school, my friends and I spent a lot of time outdoors. We played in the forests and picked berries and mushrooms under the shade of tall pine and beech trees. We watched the local people—who were called "peasants" because they were so poor—hunt for grouse, partridge, and wild ducks. Other townspeople fished for perch and pike in the swift-moving Zbrucz River.

Sometimes, on my own, I climbed a hill to the ruins of an ancient castle called the Turkish Tower, a thirteenth-century castle outside Skala. The Tower always impressed me as mysterious and romantic, and when time allowed I liked to sit on the big stone ruins and look out over Skala. In the distance, I could make out a few carriages with horses taking people to the marketplace. In summer, the Tower offered a pleasing view of surrounding fields where tomatoes, strawberries, raspberries, and cucumbers ripened on the vine. There were always troubles of one kind or another for the Jews of Skala, but life was still a blessing.

My mother, Szencia (SENT-seeya), which is Polish for Charlotte, had dark eyes, long black hair, and beautiful white teeth. She attended business school, but never liked it and ended up becoming her parents' housekeeper. She called herself Cinderella, because among her parents' five children she was the one who always did the cleaning. After marrying my father, she continued as Cinderella, caring for me and my brother, Arthur, keeping our home clean and preparing all the meals.

My father, Benjamin Gottesfeld, was a handsome man with gray eyes and black hair, and he was generous and kind. If a poor person came to him for help, my father sent him to my mother with a message such as "Your husband said to give me a coat." My father was trained as an engineer, but there wasn't much construction going on in our part of Poland, so he ended up running a hardware store. He didn't have much of a head for business. The hardware store eventually closed because he let too many customers buy things on credit, which they never paid.

What my father loved most was reading. He was a scholar who believed in the importance of education and could recite long passages of books from memory. Once a month or so, a small group of intellectuals gathered in our house to ask my father for advice and hear him read from one of his books. To own a book was a big deal in those days. Our home was filled with my father's books in French, Russian, German, Polish, Hebrew, and Yiddish. The books were big volumes with heavy cardboard covers that smelled like tree bark. As a little girl, I would carefully take down one book at a time, find a quiet place outside, and read each one as best I could. He encouraged me to read as much as I liked, but not everyone in our family agreed with him.

"Fanya, reading is bad for the eyes," my maternal grandmother, Miriam, scolded from time to time. "Who's going to marry a girl who wears glasses?" I wasn't interested in marriage. I wanted an education. I dreamed of going to Paris to study medicine, and those books in my father's library were like my best friends, always ready to offer a useful point of view about the mysteries of the world.

*   *   *

Our lives in Skala changed dramatically when Adolf Hitler became chancellor of Germany in January 1933. After being defeated in World War I, Germany fell into an economic depression. Shops had little food or goods to sell, German money was nearly worthless, and millions of Germans were out of work. Hitler's propaganda was that Germany's troubles were the fault of Jews and other "enemies." He promised to restore Germany to glory and prosperity if the German people helped him rid the nation of these "undesirable elements."

In 1935, Hitler's Nazi party announced restrictions against Jews in Germany. Soon Jews could no longer have a telephone, a radio, or even a bicycle. Jews were forbidden to enter certain stores and restaurants. It seemed like there were more and more of these regulations every day. The many restrictions increased people's hatred toward Jews, for now anti-Semitism was legal.

Anti-Semitic newspapers in Germany and Poland spread lies about Jews killing Christian children, and our neighbors in Skala turned against us even more. No one would sell us food, and when we showed up for school, the teachers shut the door in our faces.

"Go away," they said. "Jews are no longer allowed to come to class."

We had known for some time that the danger to Jews was growing. The educated Jews of Skala had read Hitler's book *Mein Kampf,* in which he wrote about his plans for waging war against the Jews, but we didn't think he would ever succeed. Germany was the most cultured country in Europe. Germany was home to some of the greatest scholars, philosophers, and composers in the world—and here was this poorly written book that spouted fanatical nonsense. No one in our community took it seriously.

But with more restrictions imposed on us every day, life for Jews in Skala was going from bad to worse.

CHAPTER THREE

A Hole in the Ground

IN SEPTEMBER 1939, Germany invaded Poland, the first of many countries that Hitler would occupy by force. His plan was to take control of all the countries around Germany, and from then on every bit of food that Polish farmers harvested was sent to Germany. The people of Skala and other towns began to go hungry. Food became so scarce that we ate anything we could find. I remember many times dinner consisted of a small bowl of hot water with some grass and leaves that we picked in the forest.

To the east of Skala lay the vast lands of the Soviet Union, a collection of many countries controlled by the largest of them, Russia. For many months the Russians had suspected that Hitler would attack the Soviet Union, so in 1939, the Russians took the offensive. Russian troops entered Skala and took control of the town. At first, the Jews of Skala welcomed the Russians. We were so scared of what the Germans would to do to us that we greeted the Russian soldiers with excitement. We quickly learned, however, that hatred of Jews was the same whether it came from Germany to the west or Russia to the east.

Soon after arriving in Skala, the Russians closed all the stores and warehouses owned by Jews. The Russians kicked Jews out of their shops and made them do backbreaking forced labor in stone quarries and on construction crews. Some Jewish families were arrested and never seen again. To force us to cooperate and work for them without making trouble, the Russians hanged a Jewish "traitor" in the town square and made all the Jews of Skala watch.

In 1941, Germany broke its treaty with the Soviet Union and invaded Soviet-held territory. Skala and surrounding areas were occupied by Nazi Germany and their allies by July. One of the Germans' first decrees was that Jews had to wear a white armband with a blue Jewish star. Then they demanded that Jews give the German authorities all their valuables, including furniture, linens, china, and jewelry. These many decrees made the Ukrainian police bold in their persecution of Jews. I would watch, horrified, when the police grabbed elderly Jewish men by their beards and slapped and shoved them around. Sometimes Jewish men were taken hostage to make sure the decrees were carried out. If the decree was not carried out within a designated time—for example, to deliver all jewelry within the next two hours—the hostages were shot.

The day came when the Germans decreed that Jews were no longer allowed to keep books. Shortly after the decree was announced, soldiers stormed into our house and began searching for books. We had hidden my father's books in the attic, but it didn't take the soldiers long to find them. The soldiers carried all my father's beautiful books down to the kitchen and spilled them across the floor. The officer in charge ripped the covers off the books and trampled on the pages, scattering them across the room. It was more than my father could bear. With tears on his face he stepped forward and tried to save some of the books. The officer in charge picked up one of the larger books and started beating my father. The jagged edges of the pages cut my father's cheeks and forehead. My father wept, but what could he do against such a bully?

"Jewish pig!" the officer yelled. "Today losing your

books makes you cry. Just wait. Soon it will be losing your lives that will make you cry."

And soon the order did indeed come for the police to round up every Jew for deportation. Why the non-Jewish people of Skala agreed to cooperate with the Nazis is complicated. Of course, many of our neighbors hated Jews even before the Germans arrived. But another reason was that many Ukrainians believed Germany would give the Ukrainian people political independence if they helped Germany win the war. It was a lie, but a useful one for getting the Ukrainians to cooperate, and so it was that for the next several years we Jews suffered at the hands of our own townspeople.

On that cold night in September 1942 when my family hid in a hole under the egg-packing warehouse, we were terrified that the police would find us and send us to a concentration camp to be tortured and shot. A few had managed to escape from the camps, and they returned to Skala with reports of Jews being murdered. Those were the images that haunted us now as we ran and hid wherever we could.

The morning after hiding in the hole, when at last

it seemed safe, I climbed out and ran with my mother, father, and brother back to my grandparents' house. We hurried inside and shut the door. A few minutes later, the door swung open. We were terrified that the police had followed us, but when we saw who it was we sighed with relief. There stood Jan, a handsome Ukrainian policeman who had recently become a friend of our family.

I was fifteen when Jan and I first met in the Skala marketplace. My family had heard that a farmer was coming with cucumbers, and my mother sent me to buy some. When I arrived at the market I found out the cucumbers were all rotten, but food was so scarce that people were trampling over me to get them first. Just then, Jan, this good-looking Ukrainian with a rifle, came up to me and said, "Let me help you." He walked up to the farmer's truck and came back to me with a bag full of cucumbers.

After that Jan began visiting me in my parents' home. Clearly he liked me, and he always arrived with gifts: a little sugar or flour for my mother, eggs for me and my brother, an aspirin or other medicine for my father. One day Jan even brought a jar of buttermilk for my grandmother. She nearly fainted when he walked up to her and politely touched his cap as he handed her the jar. She was shocked.

"Can you imagine?" my grandmother told us later. "He touched his cap—to an old Jewish woman!"

When the other policemen in his station found out about these visits, they began calling Jan a "Jewish uncle," which was intended as an insult. The phrase meant someone who loved Jews. Most of these other police were peasant boys who thought it was glamorous to carry a rifle, put on an armband, and intimidate the Jews. Jan was tall and strong, so they never dared do more than occasionally poke fun at him for having a Jewish girlfriend.

After Jan had visited us several times, I thought I was falling in love with him. But what did I know about love? My only impressions of love at age eighteen came from books by Dostoyevsky, Tolstoy, Zola, and other romantic writers. Still, I did feel something for him, and it was clear he felt something for me, as he continued to protect my family and bring us gifts.

One day Jan arrived and told us the Germans had ordered the Ukrainian police to shoot any Jews who seemed sick or weak. The remaining Jews of Skala were to be sent by train to the death camp Belzec. At that time, we didn't know much about Belzec, other than that no one ever came out of there alive.

"You must leave here before the Germans find you," Jan insisted. "Come with me. I will hide you in my house."

"Help us first get back to our home," my father pleaded, "so that we can collect some clothes and food."

With Jan leading the way, my mother, father, brother, and I left my grandparents' place and set out for our own home.

Later we heard rumors that all the Jews sent to the Belzec death camp were gassed and their bodies were buried.

CHAPTER FOUR

A Forbidden Relationship

ON THE ROAD HOME we found the bodies of people who had been shot in the roundup. We saw dozens of others bleeding from German or Ukrainian bullets. We passed crying children searching in vain for parents who had been taken away. Through smashed windows we saw dead bodies sprawled on beds and chairs. People's clothing and furniture were gone, taken by looters. Finally, we reached our house. The doors were broken, and glass from the windows lay shattered on the ground. Everything of value in the house was gone. All our food had been stolen. Whatever was left of our possessions lay ripped or broken on the wooden floor. It was useless to stay in our own home any longer. We needed someplace else to hide.

That night Jan brought us to the barn adjoining his family's house, a ten-minute walk from our home.

There we climbed up a ladder and hid in the barn's attic. He had spent many nights building a hiding place. There was just enough space for us to hide between the real wall of the attic and a false one that Jan had installed. In that space he had put a small stool, some hay that would serve as our bed, and a metal pot that we could use for a toilet.

Jan's mother and sister knew about his friendship with me and my family and had forbidden him to bring us onto their property. Jan had nonetheless brought us to his home without telling them and kept us alive with food he stole from his mother's kitchen. Thanks to his kindness we were able to eat and to stay hidden, and maybe we might even survive.

Jan was tall and handsome, and he found me attractive, even though I had never considered myself pretty. In some other country, at some other time, perhaps our attraction for each other might have been acceptable, but at that time helping Jews was a crime, and Jan's interest in me could land him in prison or worse.

From my side, I was also breaking rules by having Jan as a friend. My parents were Orthodox Jews. Less religious Jews mixed freely with non-Jews, but Orthodox Jewish parents such as mine strictly forbade their children from dating a non-Jew like Jan. Doing so was not only considered immoral but also dangerous. We Jews had no power or influence in Skala. The Jewish people did not yet have a nation of their own. We protected ourselves by staying away from non-Jews. We considered non-Jews dangerous because most of them hated us, and a Jewish girl who was friendly with a non-Jew risked being shunned by the entire Jewish community.

But what choice did I have? Here was a policeman who was willing to bring us food and protect us from harm.

"Fanya, be nice to Jan," my father told me.

What did he mean, "be nice"? Was he telling me it was okay to be romantic with Jan? In those days, we broke a lot of rules and did what was necessary to stay alive. Hunger made us desperate. Some nights, my father and I crept into wealthier people's gardens and took some rotten pears or apples off the ground. Technically we were stealing, which was immoral, but under such emergency conditions, words such as "moral" and "ethical" took on different meanings. When your life is threatened, the usual standards of right and wrong don't necessarily apply.

CHAPTER FIVE

Winter 1942–43—A Bottle of Vodka or a Pair of Boots

WHEN WINTER ARRIVED Jan's barn was too cold for us to stay there, so he brought me and my family to the home of Christian next-door neighbors who agreed to hide us. That was a brave thing for them to do. If the police discovered someone hiding Jews, they set fire to their house and burned everyone in it alive.

"Do you hate the Germans as much as I do?" I asked Jan.

"I hate the misery they cause," he said. His answer made me think carefully about the nature of hate, who it is directed at, and why. In those terrible days, there were a few non-Jews in Skala who, in exchange for money, hid Jews. They were also taking big risks. Was I supposed to hate them, too, because they only helped if Jews paid them?

It was a relief when Jan's neighbors agreed to hide

us, but they set down strict rules. We had to stay hidden inside the house and were not allowed outside, even to draw water from their well. Consequently, Arthur and I could never take a bath, and we lived in constant filth. The lice in our clothes and hair were so thick we had to spend hours each day picking them out and crushing them between our fingers.

We looked and smelled like wild animals, but there was no choice. We never kept a light on after dark for fear of attracting the attention of neighbors who would gladly turn us in to the Germans. The police offered a reward for turning in a Jew: a bottle of vodka or a pair of leather boots. That's what a Jew's life was worth in those days.

The German officers and Ukrainian police conducted raids without notice. One Sunday morning, we heard them coming: dogs barking and men yelling. We ran from the house and scattered in all directions. I remembered that not too far away lived a Ukrainian man who had gone to school with my uncle. I ran to his house and pounded on the door until he opened it.

"Please," I pleaded, "let me stay for a few hours."

The man was wearing his best clothes and hat and was obviously about to go to church, so I tried appealing to his Christian charity. I dropped to my knees, folded my hands like I was praying, and said, "If they find me, you can say you didn't know I was here."

The man just shook his head. "No," he said. Then he pointed a finger at me and said, "You killed Jesus Christ. Your people murdered our Lord. I can't sit in church and pray knowing you are here." He pushed me away, locked the door, and walked off.

I sneaked back through the forest to the home of Jan's neighbors, thinking deeply about what this man had said. How had he come to hate us so much? Had he always hated us and simply pretended to be my uncle's friend when they were classmates? On the other hand, maybe he was just pretending to hate us so the neighbors would consider him a loyal Nazi. But what if he really did hate us? Should I show him the compassion I hoped he would show me and my family? These were my thoughts as I crept back to the house of Jan's neighbors.

By the time I arrived the roundup was over and it was safe to enter the house. That night I asked Jan, "Do you think Jews killed Jesus Christ?"

He took my hand and answered, "How should I know? I wasn't there."

"My family wasn't there, either," I said. "We weren't even alive then, so they can't blame us, but they do." I was close to tears. "Do you hate me?" I asked him.

"Would I be sitting here with you if I did?" he said.

There was something in his eyes I had never seen before. He was looking at me with pity. It was the first time I saw just how torn Jan was by his feelings for me.

CHAPTER SIX

The Sound of Boots

IN THE MIDDLE OF THE NIGHT, my family and I were awakened by the sound of boots outside the house where we were hiding. It was another raid; another *Aktion*.

"Take Fanya and go!" my father pleaded with Jan. "I will look out for the rest of my family."

Jan grabbed my hand, and we ran quietly out of the house. He took me through a back road to a hiding place he had prepared behind a bathtub in my grandparents' yard. We crawled behind the bathtub and lay down together. Jan gave me his arm as a pillow.

A moment later, I had a terrible attack of cramps. I writhed in agony, trying desperately not to cry out and give away our location. Spasms of pain racked my body, and I thought I was going to die. Jan held me in his arms and steadied me until the cramps subsided and I could sit up. After a few minutes, the spasms stopped.

Jan had just seen me at my worst, yet he remained calm and detached, like a doctor. His only concern was for my comfort. It is easy to care for someone who is healthy and attractive, and another thing altogether to help someone who is so sick as to be repulsive. My respect for Jan had never been deeper.

The next morning Jan crept out of the hole and came back with a small can of warm milk. He took off the cover and held the milk to my mouth, and I drank. It had been months since I had had any milk. It tasted like honey, sweet and warm. I will never forget that drink of milk.

When night fell, we ventured out and crept silently through the forest, back to my parents' house. They had managed to return home without being caught. Once inside, I bent down to kiss my sleeping little brother.

Winter passed, each day merging into the next, with little change to make the time go by. Sometimes, as I lay awake at night, I told myself, *I want to live. I want to accomplish something before I die.* But how long would I live? We waited, not knowing when we would hear the sound of the next *Aktion,* the clop of leather boots, or the firing of guns. If I had to die, I hoped it would come quickly.

My father and Jan spent weeks reviewing the names of every gentile (non-Jew) they knew in Skala and the surrounding towns and discussed the best options for hiding from the police. There were critical questions to be answered. Where was the safest place to hide? In the forest? In someone's basement? If we tried to stay together, whose home could we hide in? Whom could we trust to not give us up to the police? Would we be safer separating and hiding in different places?

My father's preference was the home of Sidor Sokolowski, a poor Christian farmer who lived with his wife and daughter in the nearby tiny town of Trujce (Troo-YIT-za). My father had once worked with Sidor on the construction crew of a bridge. When Sidor was falsely blamed for an error in the construction, my father spoke up and protected him from punishment. Their friendship had been strong ever since. Sidor's wife was a Ukrainian woman named Marynka, and they had a daughter named Hania. Sidor and his family lived in a small house with a small patch of land. Perhaps, my father told Jan, we could do chores as payment if Sidor agreed to hide us.

"Go with Jan," my father told me, "then come back and tell me if you think we can all hide there. In particular, we need to know what kind of person Sidor's wife is. Will she turn us over to the authorities? Watch their little girl, Hania, and decide if she is trustworthy or whether she might give us away by accident. And is there enough space for the four of us? Look carefully, then come back and let us know."

The Ukrainian police had given the Germans a list of Jews who were still in hiding, and the *Aktionen* continued. All day long German soldiers burst into people's homes unannounced, but the night finally came when there were no soldiers in sight and Jan and I could risk running to Sidor's home. I wrapped a thick shawl around my head and lined my jacket with paper to keep out the nighttime chill. Jan held my hand, and we moved silently through the forest.

Jan and I reached Sidor's house, and I knocked on the door. Sidor opened it. His face had an expression of great concern. In those days, someone knocking at your door at night usually meant trouble. I quickly explained that I was the daughter of his old friend Benjamin Gottesfeld.

Sidor nodded with relief and politely welcomed us inside. He looked to be in his late forties, with dark hair and deep-set eyes, and I was struck by his kind voice and hospitality. He showed us to a tiny alcove, where he invited us to rest. Jan sat on the floor with his back to the wall. I lay down on a wooden bench covered by a quilt so worn you could see your hand through it, and closed my eyes.

When I woke up, it was morning. I sat up and saw Jan seated with Sidor at the kitchen table. I noticed for the first time just how poor Sidor and his family were. Their whole house was this one room. A cast-iron stove with a dented tin chimney covered most of one wall of the room. Smoke from a wood fire wafted up through the chimney and out into a bright morning sky. Sunlight filtered into the room through an open wood-framed window. A square chest with two drawers and knotty wooden handles sat along the opposite wall, flanked by a couple of worn wooden chairs.

Close to where I sat was a bed covered with a threadbare blanket. A few kitchen utensils, tattered quilts, a small trunk—these were the sum total of Sidor's household goods. It was clear that cooking, eating, sleeping, and socializing were all done in this one small room.

Sidor's wife, Marynka, sat on the bed, pulling on thick stockings and looking at us with suspicion. Clearly she was not happy to have us there. I didn't blame her. Food was scarce, and if her husband, Sidor, agreed to hide us, no doubt it meant giving some of their own food to feed us. Hiding behind her mother and watching us was their daughter, Hania. I guessed she was about eight years old, my brother's age. She had long blond hair like her mother's and dark eyes like her father's.

Sidor handed me a cup of hot water flavored with barley flour, which was what passed for coffee during the war years. "We're going to the market," he told me. "Don't go near the windows. Don't open the door to anyone, and don't light a fire. The neighbors will see the smoke. We will be back by nightfall."

Sidor and his family picked up woven straw baskets and headed out the door. Jan and I were left alone. We mounted a ladder to the attic, spread armfuls of hay across the wooden planks of the attic floor, and fell fast asleep.

CHAPTER SEVEN

A Father's Prediction

BY MY THIRD DAY IN SIDOR'S HOME, it was clear Marynka would let me stay but not my brother or our parents. The risk of so many people would be too great. Just a few days before in a neighboring town, German soldiers found a Christian man who had hidden a family of Jews in his house. The soldiers made him watch as they shot his wife and children along with the Jews.

Sidor tried to pacify his wife. "Fanya's father has always treated me well," he said. "When the time comes, rest assured that Benjamin and his family will be as good to us as we are to them now."

The next night, I returned with Jan to my parents, who were still hiding in his barn. I was ready to give them my report, but as soon as I walked in I saw my mother in tears and a hurt look on my father's face that I will never forget. They had just received word that my father's parents had been caught in an *Aktion* and killed. I loved my grandparents, and this news was a terrible shock, but there was no time to grieve their deaths. The Nazis were closing in. I helped my mother and father pack what few possessions we could carry, and we quickly headed to Sidor's house.

Sidor's wife was at the door, scowling at us. Sidor gently moved her aside and helped us climb a ladder to their attic.

Our routine in Sidor's attic was the same as when Jan and I had been there on our own. My father, mother, brother, and I had to be completely quiet all day. There was no room to walk, so my father constantly shifted his weight back and forth and jiggled his legs to keep the blood circulating. At night, when there was less risk of anyone visiting, we were allowed to come down to exercise. We walked back and forth on the hard wood floor, chatting about trivial things, until some of our leg stiffness began to subside. Then we climbed back up to the attic and fell once again into silence.

In the morning, before Marynka and Sidor left to work in the fields, they gave us each a small slice of bread. Often, that was all we had to eat for the entire day. The extreme hunger we felt is hard to describe. Imagine an emptiness in your stomach so complete that you get cramps and headaches and feel so dizzy you can't think straight. On those rare days when Jan was able to visit us, he often brought bits of food: a pocketful of cornmeal, a small sausage, maybe some cheese. Then he left, and the hunger returned.

The pain of hunger and headaches would have been bearable if there were something to do. But there wasn't. We sat, stared at the walls, and sometimes talked about the food we used to have. The monotony was torture. To distract us from such terrible thoughts, my father recited lessons from history or passages from novels he had read during his university days, and we talked about them. Sometimes he chanted portions of the Torah, and we joined in as best we could.

We knew better than to complain. Our hardships were not like those of Jews who had been sent to camps to be beaten and murdered. So far, at least, my family and I had not been subjected to such horrors. Still, we did have nightmares about what could happen to us.

From time to time, my father looked at me and said, "Fanya, you will survive. I can see it."

Was he a psychic? Or were such prophecies just wishful thinking from a frightened parent? There was a word in German, *überleben,* which meant surviving despite the odds. Each day I thought, "I must try to live one more day, despite the odds."

CHAPTER EIGHT

"You Have to Leave"

OVER THE WEEKS AND MONTHS that my family and I hid in Sidor and Marynka's attic, we heard them argue about how long they should let us stay. Marynka resented us being there at all, since hiding Jews could get them all killed. At first she seemed willing to help keep our presence a secret and even told Hania to never mention us in school or in church. And Hania never did. The only time I ever heard her speak of us was to her family's German shepherd, Rex. "Don't tell anyone about the people in the barn," she warned him, "or my mother will cook you in the soup."

Other times, it was clear Marynka could not stand our being in her home. She would throw a shoe or broom against the wall and yell at her husband for putting his own family in such danger. Sidor did his best to calm her down.

"He's a good man," Sidor said, referring to my father. "I can't send him to his grave."

"Instead, you're digging ours!" Marynka yelled, and then she threw a kettle against the wall.

We listened to these fights with growing concern. Marynka had every right to be upset. Our presence in her home was a serious danger, and my father and Jan anticipated that sometime soon she would force Sidor to make us leave. So my father and Jan built a new hiding place, this time behind a chicken coop attached to Sidor's barn.

The chicken coop was a three-foot-high box made of wooden boards nailed together and covered with a slanted tin roof. The space was only wide enough for two people to sit comfortably. There were four of us, and we squeezed in only with great effort. The roof was too low to stand upright, and there was not enough room to lie down. Still, in this new hiding place we would be less of a risk to Sidor and his wife and daughter, since we would not be in their house if the police came looking for us.

The small wooden structure stood against the outside of the barn. On the other side, inside the barn, was a feeding trough for the cows. We entered the hiding place between the barn and the chicken coop by going into the barn, crawling underneath the trough, and squeezing into the small space between the outside wall and the chicken coop.

When my brother, mother, father, and I did a test, we squirmed snakelike on our bellies under the trough, through the hole in the barn wall, and into the hiding space, where we pressed tightly together. Wind howled through the cracks in the wooden walls, and we dared not imagine what it would be like in winter. Once we finished practicing how to get into and out of the space behind the chicken coop, we returned to the attic in Sidor's house.

Early one morning, Sidor's Rex started barking. I peered outside through a chink in the attic wall and saw German soldiers jumping out of cars and motorcycles. Ukrainian police followed them with rifles. "They're coming!" I whispered to my parents and brother.

We jumped down from the attic, ran to the barn, and quickly squirmed under the trough and into the hiding space behind the chicken coop. Moments later, the Germans stormed into the barn and ordered the soldiers to search everywhere. We heard neighbors outside the barn, laughing and cheering on the soldiers. It was as if they were making a holiday of waiting for us to be found and shot. I told myself this was it, only a matter of minutes before they found us, and once again I prayed that when the time came they would kill us quickly.

The Germans ordered the Ukrainians to dig holes in every part of the barn. For hours, we listened to the *chink-chink* of shovels digging through the hay that covered the floor of the barn and into the hard-packed dirt, searching for places where we might be hiding. Several hours later, there was silence.

We waited. By morning, the only sounds were birds chirping in the fields and trees, and it seemed like the Germans and their Ukrainian helpers were gone. Still, we agreed it was not yet time to come out from behind the chicken coop. What if the Germans were only pretending to have left? What if they were waiting to grab us as soon as we emerged?

A few hours after dark, Sidor entered the barn and cleared away the dirt and hay that covered the entrance to our hiding place. We crawled out from the hole under the trough, amazed at still being alive. Sidor hugged each of us and crossed himself. "It's a miracle," he said over and over. "I expected to find you dead."

That evening, he returned to the barn and handed us a whole loaf of bread. "You have to leave," he said. "Rumor has it the Germans are coming back tomorrow." Then he handed my father a blanket.

"It's cold in the forest," he said. "I will take you there."

CHAPTER NINE

Autumn
1943—Resistance

WE PREPARED TO LEAVE FOR THE FOREST. Our shoes had long ago fallen apart; to replace them, my mother, father, brother, and I tied rags around our feet. Around midnight, Sidor led us through the forest, down back roads, and through fields dotted with stacks of hay. It was fall. Dried leaves carpeted the banks of the Zbrucz River and crunched underfoot. We took turns carrying Arthur, who had gone limp from fear and merely stared out as if hypnotized. It was still dark three hours later when we arrived at a line of trees bordering a dense wood. Sidor said good-bye, turned, and returned home.

We made our way through a thicket of pine trees and came to a clearing. In the moonlight, we saw someone following us. A friend? An enemy? He approached and said he was a scout working for Jews who were hiding in the forest. He recognized my father and shook his hand enthusiastically. Turning to all of us, he said, "Follow me."

After an hour, the scout stopped. In the dim light of moon and stars, we watched people emerge from holes dug in the ground. There were dozens of these dugouts, and from what I could see each hole was big enough for three or four people. The tops of the holes were level with the forest floor and had been camouflaged with branches and leaves.

The scout told us that about 150 Jews from Skala and from shtetls (small villages) in the surrounding area had fled to this part of the forest. Hiding in these underground dugouts was their last hope of escaping capture.

Word spread that we had arrived. People climbed out of their bunkers, smiling and clapping their hands on hearing that my father was still alive.

"He's here!" they cried out. "Benjamin Gottesfeld is here!"

I knew my father had been highly respected by the Jews of Skala for his vast learning, but I'd had no idea how much until that moment. One man who must have known my father well in Skala ran up and said, "Mr. Gottesfeld, if you have managed to survive, we can all hope to see the end of war."

My father had nothing to do with how long the war would last, but desperate people grasp at straws. The man led my father to a bunker, where a group of older people asked him questions about the Russian advance. The Soviet Union was a powerful country with a big army. If the Soviets succeeded in defeating the Germans, we could at last go home.

"How far away are the Russians?" the partisans asked my father. "How strong are their forces?"

My father told them whatever he knew from Jan's reports and from things he had heard the neighbors say outside our hiding place, but in truth he didn't know much. Most of what my father had heard was only rumors. Still, he didn't want to disappoint the partisans, so he made his description of the Russian advance as optimistic as possible.

That night we watched a group of men and boys assemble in the darkness and quietly head out of the forest toward towns in the surrounding area. We were told they were going to look for food. The people hiding in the forest were starving. Many had already died of hunger, and there was no choice now but to risk everything. The nighttime raiders headed out after midnight and crept into any house or farm they came across. Some raiders succeeded in stealing a few vegetables or scraps from someone's garbage pile. Others were caught by German or Ukrainian police and killed.

Someone hugged me from behind. I turned, and there was Lotka, a friend I had known in school in Skala. As a little girl, Lotka had always been nicely dressed, her long brown hair always neatly combed. She looked so different now. Instead of the prim and proper girl I had known, here stood a young woman. She was dressed in rags, pine needles and leaves stuck to her hair, and she looked more mature than I remembered from our school days.

"The dugouts are different sizes," she explained, "depending on how many people live in them. Every few weeks, if we get hints that the Ukrainians are becoming too aware of our presence, we move to another part of the forest."

"What do you eat?" I asked her.

"We store up rainwater," she replied, "then we pick wild mushrooms or forest plants and cook a little soup. We only make a fire for cooking late at night when it's too dark for people to see the smoke."

She led me to her bunker, where I met our old classmate Rubcio (ROOB-chee-o). I once had a crush on this husky, good-looking boy, but he had always preferred Lotka. They described how the people living in the forest built their bunkers by digging with their hands and using small trees and dry branches to hide the roofs.

"Just walking here to our bunker," Rubcio said, "you probably walked over the heads of a dozen people without even knowing it."

"We're starting a Jewish partisan group," Rubcio said. "Why don't you join us?"

Partisans were armed groups that worked in secret to harass the enemy. Partisans were mostly young men and some women who had escaped capture by the Nazis and hid in forests and mountains. From their hiding places the partisans mounted attacks on German arms depots, stole supplies, and did whatever damage to the Nazis they could with their meager cache of weapons.

To my mind Lotka, Rubcio, and the others in this desolate part of the forest were heroes. They had done more than merely run away from an enemy. They were rebels defying the odds, taking action rather than surrendering to death. I doubt any of them thought they would actually defeat the Germans. I doubt any of them even thought they all would survive their time in the forest. But here was real *überleben* in action. They may have known that many were going to die, but at least they were doing something, and that inspired me.

When we heard the word "resistance," most people thought about fighting the Germans with a weapon. But there were many other kinds of resistance. During my time in hiding, we heard of religious Jews who continued to pray even after being sent to the camps, where prayer was strictly forbidden. Other kinds of resistance included secretly printing and distributing reports that warned people about what the Germans were doing and provided information on how to stay alive. Printing or distributing such reports was punishable by death. Jews resisted in other ways, too—for example, by continuing to educate their children in underground schools, staging artistic and cultural events, escaping deportation, and staging revolts inside the camps.

How inspiring it was to meet people who pushed on even when there seemed to be little hope of succeeding. That impulse to keep trying no matter the consequences amazed me. Jan's acts of kindness toward me and my family, for example, could easily have gotten him killed. Sidor hiding us in his home could have gotten his whole family killed. Who can explain such extraordinary actions? Lotka and Rubcio planned to form a small fighting force, and there was something righteous in them that I would remember the rest of my life.

Despite his admiration for the partisans in the forest, my father refused to let us stay with them. "Staying here will be our death," he insisted. "Jews who stay together in such numbers are more easily found. They are inviting their own destruction."

Reluctantly, we all agreed to leave the forest early the next morning.

CHAPTER TEN

The Death of a Friend

WE WERE ASLEEP IN OUR HOLE IN THE GROUND when all of a sudden we heard rifle shots and screams. I could feel the pounding of feet above our heads. I looked over the edge of our bunker and saw people running in all directions in the pre-dawn light.

Gunfire erupted around us. Bullets whizzed by with a sound like angry wasps. Hand grenades exploded so close to our hole that the ground shook and we smelled burnt gunpowder. Grenades came soaring through the air and exploded inside bunkers to our left and right. German and Ukrainian police were running everywhere with bayonets fixed on their rifles. They were kicking aside coverings over the dugouts and throwing into them armfuls of smoking, burning straw. The people trapped inside the burning holes screamed. Voices yelled out in

German and Ukrainian, "Come out, Jews! You cannot escape!"

Surely this was it. We were all going to die.

I held on to my parents and brother. We balled ourselves up against the wall of our bunker. The explosions went on forever, it seemed. Then all at once they stopped. Hours passed. I brushed aside branches and leaves and looked out over the edge of our hole in the ground. The soldiers had left. Dead bodies lay everywhere. Almost all the Jews in the forest had been killed.

I closed my eyes. Death was frightening. I climbed out and crawled over to Lotka and Rubcio's bunker. They were gone. Had they managed to run away? Were they still alive? I scrambled back down into the hole and told my parents what I had seen. Then I crawled into their laps and was so overcome by fear that I fell fast asleep.

In the morning a shadow fell across my face and woke me. It was Jan. Once he saw that I was alive, he went over to see what had happened to my brother and parents. He blinked in surprise. They weren't hurt. Somehow, miraculously, all four of us had survived the raid. We stared at one another in disbelief.

Jan explained that he had gone to Sidor's home to check on us and learned that we had gone to the forest. He turned to my father and offered to bring us back to the attic of his barn and once again hide us there. My father gratefully accepted.

Jan brought me first, then he returned to the forest and hours later came back, climbed the wooden ladder, and handed up my brother. Arthur was limp. I studied his face, which was expressionless, and it terrified me. I put him on a pile of straw, and he lay there breathing but not moving, just staring. The gunfire and killing had traumatized him, and he was in shock. Jan climbed up the wooden ladder and sat next to me in the attic of the barn. I asked him if he knew what had happened to Lotka and Rubcio. Jan's face went gray.

"The Germans captured them," he said. "Your friends were taken with others to a spot in the forest. The Germans forced them to dig their own graves. Then the soldiers shot them."

Through the slats in the attic wall, we heard a group of Jan's neighbors talking outside.

"Did they get that swine, Benjamin Gottesfeld?" one asked.

"Not yet, but don't worry," another said. "We'll get him and his family when they come back."

That night Jan handed me a note that my friend Lotka had given him before the raid. In the note she wrote, "It was wonderful to see you in the forest. Remember me as your good friend. Love, Lotka." I stared in silence at the walls of Jan's attic and wondered what Lotka had felt in those final moments before she was shot.

CHAPTER ELEVEN

December 1943—
The Edge of Death

FOR THE NEXT TWO WEEKS, Jan traveled from one town to another, looking for anyone who would agree to take me and my family into their home and hide us for a while. Everyone turned him away. Some spit at him when they realized what he was asking them to do. Hide Jews? Was he crazy? "You're as bad as they are," they yelled.

Jan managed to find a few potatoes and a jug of water, then he came back, gave us the food, and told us the news. There was no place else for us to go. We would have to remain in the attic of his family's barn.

On top of all the other troubles he was going through on our behalf, Jan's family suspected he was hiding us. They had already known for some time that he was fond of me, that he had his "little Jew girl" somewhere. Why else did he travel out so often at night, if not to bring food to her and her family? They hated him for exposing his own family to such risk.

Jan lied. He denied he was hiding anyone. He had lost interest in me, he lied, and if he went out so often it was to chase other girls. I doubted his family believed him, but there was nothing they could say to change his mind—and miraculously so far they had not discovered us hiding in the attic of their barn.

Jan went through so much for us, but some part of me knew we could never get married. The differences between us were just too great. He was a non-Jew and a policeman whose job was to hunt down Jews and kill them. Even if we did survive the war, the ignorant people of Skala would still hate Jews, and they would make our life together miserable. Besides, he had little education and no ambition to live abroad or study anything. Those were my dreams, not his, and I had them all the time. How could I ever ignore the differences between us?

Arthur peeked through a crack in the attic wall and pointed. A man was coming. It was Sidor. He burst into the barn and grinned.

"Italy has surrendered!" he said. "Do you know what this means? It means Germany will lose the war!" Then he did a little dance around the floor.

Italy had been fighting on the side of Germany, but in September 1943, Italy had surrendered to the Allies. Maybe Sidor was right, and the war was coming to an end. So certain was Sidor of this change in our fortunes that he invited us to return to the hiding place behind the chicken coop of his barn. He could bring us food there until we could walk out as free people. Surely, despite the odds, that day would come soon.

But freedom is never that easy. We returned to Sidor's home and once more crawled back into that tiny, filthy space behind the chicken coop. Sidor spread fresh straw in the hiding place. Then he gave us an old, ripped-up quilt and covered the entry hole inside the barn with bricks and hay, but it was still the same tight fit. We sat squeezed together against the wooden walls, unable to lie down or turn sideways without everyone turning together. There was no way we could know that the war was far from over, and that we would be in that cramped, rat-infested hole for months.

Days stretched into weeks. The winter of 1943 turned bitter cold. My hands and feet were always numb, yet I sweated all the time from being pressed up against my mother, father, and brother. It was painful being both cold and hot, like plunging into ice water when you have a fever.

Some days Sidor or Marynka came by with potato peels or other scraps for us to eat, but other days we went hungry. The metal pot we used for a toilet filled up. If we changed places too quickly, we knocked it over and soiled the straw with our waste. The lice multiplied, fed off the filth, crawled through our hair and clothing, and gnawed at our skin. There were so many lice on my head that my hair was moving. We relied on touch to pick the lice off our bodies, but it was a losing battle. There were just too many. Our tiny hiding place behind the chicken coop was a dark, smelly, lice-infested garbage pail.

Under such conditions and for such a long time, it was inevitable that we would become sick. I was the first. It started as a fever that got progressively worse. It lasted for weeks. My fever went higher and higher, and I finally blacked out. I was in a coma-like state for some time. During those days, I remember waking only once or twice, always with an agonizing thirst, then lapsing back into unconsciousness.

Four weeks later the fever finally broke. When I woke up I was hungrier than I had ever been in my life. I used to think of hunger as a little mouse gnawing at my stomach. Now it was a huge dog that chewed on my body and mind.

It was impossible to think of how my brother or parents felt, so preoccupied was I with my own suffering. The hungrier and sicker we became, the more my father worked to keep us alert by reciting passages from renowned authors such as Goethe, Schiller, or Shakespeare. Sometimes he recounted extensive portions of novels by Polish or Yiddish writers.

To keep our spirits up, my father tried to describe the good life we would have after the war. "We will all go to Paris," he said, nodding his head, "and there will be pretty clothes and plenty to eat. For you, Fanya, there will be medical school. You must promise me that you will teach your children Hebrew and Shakespeare."

I loved my father for his faith in the future and for his hope in a time when words such as "art," "culture," and "education" would once again mean something. Assuring me about one day going to Paris was a noble gesture on his part, but for all we knew it was just wishful thinking.

Christmas Eve 1943 came, and Sidor took a big risk by inviting us into his home for a small party. After midnight, when it was less dangerous to come out of hiding, we moved quickly and quietly from the chicken coop to his house. Jan carried Arthur from the barn, since Arthur's legs had grown too thin and weak to support him.

Marynka heated a pot of water on their iron stove, and my mother washed Arthur and then her own neck and chest. My father took his turn with the hot water. Then I washed my face and hands and chest for the first time in months. It felt so good that I cried. Hania held up a sheet as a screen while I dried myself.

"I wish you could come live in the house again," Hania whispered to me. "Then I wouldn't be so afraid."

"Afraid of what?" I whispered back.

"My mother says the Germans will come for you," Hania replied, "and when they do, they will shoot all of us and burn down the house. She says they will shoot Rex, too." Her young mind tried to grasp the idea of being shot. "I have seen farmers kill cows and pigs and chickens," she said. "They use a knife. But a bullet makes such a small hole. Does it hurt when the blood comes out?"

I tied the sheet around me, hugged her, and reminded her that it was Christmas. All the soldiers were at home celebrating with their families, and she had nothing to fear.

Sidor started the Christmas party by passing around a dusty bottle of vodka he had been saving. We took small sips and toasted one another: Sidor and his Christian family, and we, his hidden Jews who had never celebrated Christmas. Hania tried to amuse my brother. She took a small wooden top and spun it on the floor in front of him. Arthur ignored her and stared forward without expression. He had not smiled in a long time.

Marynka had managed to purchase a small bag of flour and some sugar. She mixed the flour with water and kneaded the mixture with her hands until it became a ball of dough. Then she tore off small bits of dough and rolled them into small flat pancakes. She fried them in a pot of oil on her stove, then stacked the pancakes on the table and sprinkled them with the sugar. We ate so many pancakes that we all had stomachaches afterward. Even Rex couldn't eat any more. The party ended with another toast to freedom and an end to the war. My mother stood up and raised her glass.

Oh no, I thought. *My mother hates Marynka. I'm sure she's going to say something nasty about her.*

"Let us drink to Sidor and his family," my mother said. "May they have a healthy Christmas. And let us hope that the ring of dirt we left after bathing with their water pail is not too hard to scrub off!"

Everybody laughed and applauded. I was astonished. It was the first time any of us had laughed since coming to Sidor and Marynka's house—and it was my mother who had cracked the joke! We thanked our hosts, walked quickly back to the barn, and crawled once more into our tiny space behind the chicken coop.

That night the wind turned freezing cold. We huddled close together to stay warm. Rats scudded in and out of the smelly straw.

CHAPTER TWELVE

——————

1944—Losing Jan

JANUARY WAS BRUTALLY COLD. Peering through cracks in the wooden slats of the chicken coop, I watched snow race across the fields and pile up higher and higher until trees resembled white soldiers. The wind wailed so loudly that it sounded like a pack of wolves, and we could not hear one another speak. Sidor and Marynka came only every few days with food, and each time the little bowl of soup was smaller and the pieces of bread thinner. We had eaten so little that we looked like skeletons. I did not think we would live much longer.

One morning Sidor came to get my father. Through the slats of the chicken coop I could see and hear them talking together outside the barn. Sidor was saying he had lost hope that the war would end before spring. There was no food even for his own family, he said, and his wife was once more threatening to turn us in. I liked Sidor. He was a decent man, but I understood why he could no longer risk hiding us. I watched my father fall to his knees.

"Please don't kick us out, for my children's sake," my father said with pleading hands. "Don't send them to their deaths. You will see. The war will end, and we'll be like one big family."

Sidor had a heart that was easily moved. He could not bring himself to send us away to be killed. "You talk about the war ending, but it's just talk," he said, with a look that made it clear he was condemning his own family to die. Sidor slowly motioned with his hand, sending his old friend back into the hiding place behind the chicken coop.

In February the weather turned even colder. Ice crusted on the walls of our wretched hiding place, and I nearly had given up hope of surviving. Our bodies had gone numb from the cold. Our arms and legs had atrophied from lack of movement, and we spent each day in a kind of suspended state, staring, nodding off, not caring any longer about lice or rats, huddled together in a desperate attempt to stay warm. We were still breathing, but that was about it.

Jan had not come to see us in weeks. Then one evening he arrived in a horse-drawn wagon. I watched him go into Sidor and Marynka's house. After a while he came out and called to me to come out of the hiding place. I could barely move but managed to pull myself through the hole and into the barn. I stumbled behind Jan to some bales of hay, and we sat. I knew I smelled like garbage, but I was beyond caring what he or anyone else thought about me.

"I'm going out with someone else now," Jan said. "She's the daughter of my father's friend."

The news didn't surprise me. Jan was a good catch, and I was a skinny, smelly Jew. Who could blame him? He still had a life.

"What do you want me to say?" I asked him. "Congratulations?"

"Look, Fanya," he said. "I don't want to go out with anyone else. You're the one I love. But no one has anything to eat. This girl's family is well-off." He awkwardly kissed me good-bye and left. I crawled back into my hole.

"What did Jan say about the war?" my father asked. "When will he come again?"

I told him things between me and Jan were over

and that he was seeing someone else. The seriousness of this shift in our situation turned my father's face more gray than it already was. For the past three years, we had counted on Jan for food, news, and safety. However bad our situation became, a word from Jan had helped us believe there might be something more in our future than torture or slow death from starvation. Now he was gone. No more Jan, no more hope.

Sidor did his best to keep us fed, but there was barely enough food for his own family. One day he brought us a bowl of water in which beets had been boiled. "It's all I have to give you," he said in a choked voice. "Such a comfortable home you once had," he said, "and now you're starving in that rat hole with nothing to eat but beet water."

With so little food, a few days later I again fell into a coma-like state. In those rare moments when I regained consciousness I didn't know where I was. I vaguely knew that my name was Fanya and that I was twenty years old and hiding with my family. But as soon as I thought about these things, they would dissolve into a fuzzy cloud.

I had dreams that I was a little girl again, running

happily around our garden and hiding behind bushes and piles of cordwood. In these hunger-induced hallucinations, it seemed important for some reason that no one find me. From time to time I woke up from the dream and was surprised to find I was still alive.

Then I fell back into unconsciousness and drifted away.

CHAPTER THIRTEEN

The Sky Exploded

ONE DAY IN MARCH 1944, we heard a heavy rumbling. "Tanks," my father said, but we couldn't tell if they were German or Russian.

Soon after, Sidor moved aside the bales of hay that hid the opening to our hiding place and called to us. We crawled out and staggered slowly behind him to his house. When we were all inside Sidor's home and seated, he began hopping up and down.

"You should have seen them!" he squealed with delight, and then described the situation, explaining that the Russian Red Army had arrived and that the Germans were running "like dogs with their tails between their legs," he said. He and his wife knelt down in front of a picture of Jesus and gave thanks.

I was feeling less thankful. If God got the credit for ending a war, shouldn't He also get the blame for starting it? What kind of God invents Nazis? What kind of God would let me and my family starve to death? What had we ever done to Him?

"I don't believe it," I said weakly. "I don't believe the war is ending. We've been told that before. You'll see. The Germans will come back."

Sidor refused to be discouraged, and he invited us all to leave the foul hiding place and live once more in his attic. He wanted to clean out the hiding place, he said, in case anyone came poking around and found it. Somehow, I was awake enough to offer an opinion.

"You haven't been in there. Even rats can't live in that filthy place," I mumbled. "You can't clean it. The only way to clean it is with fire. Burn it down."

Arthur nodded in agreement. "Burn it," he said.

Hearing Arthur speak shocked everyone in the room. For the past three years, he had survived attacks by soldiers, bullets flying by his face, hand grenades exploding within yards of where he sat in our forest hideout, and watching people die—and all the horrors had rendered him mute.

"Burn it" were the first words he had spoken in months.

*   *   *

One morning the sky exploded. We climbed quickly down from the attic and ran outside into Sidor's yard. Above our heads, fighter planes were waging battle, shooting machine guns without stop, diving at one another with screeching sounds. Some of the planes were painted with Nazi swastikas, others with the hammer and sickle of the Soviet air force.

The planes fired at one another—*Ak-ak-ak!*—and then zoomed away. As best we could tell, the Russian planes were chasing the German planes. If the Russians could defeat Hitler's air force in aerial combat, maybe there would indeed be an end to the war.

The fighter planes eventually went their separate ways, but whatever hope we had for the war to end tomorrow did nothing to fill our empty stomachs today. My father went out looking for food. He did not come back. We waited for him. Hours turned into days. Our concern turned from anxiety to fear, and then to dread.

Where was my father?

Sidor went to the marketplace in Skala and returned with a somber expression. "People are saying your father went to Jan's home to ask for his help finding food. That was the last time anyone saw your father. My friend—your father, Benjamin—is gone. No one knows where."

My mother started crying. My brother sat mute again. I discussed with Sidor the possibilities. Could my father have been caught and taken away by the Ukrainian police? Even with Russians chasing away the Germans, a Jew was never safe. The Ukrainians still wanted the Jews dead, whether Germany lost the war or not.

"Is that what happened?" I asked. "Did the police kill my father?"

Sidor talked again about how Jan was the last one to see him, and the expression on his face frightened me. Did Jan have anything to do with my father's death? He was a policeman, after all, and responsible for rounding up Jews. Was that what happened? Did Jan kill my father?

I never found out.

A short time later, the Soviets chased the Germans out of Skala. For us in Poland, the war was over—but not our troubles. My father was gone, we had no home to return to, and our other family members were probably dead. We were lost, with nowhere to go.

CHAPTER FOURTEEN

Stolen Sandals

MY BROTHER, MOTHER, AND I no longer had to hide behind Sidor's chicken coop, where we had lived for months. With the Germans gone, it was safer to sleep on the floor of Sidor's kitchen. Yet our clothes were rags, we were dangerously underweight, food was still scarce as ever, and staying alive took serious effort.

With my father gone and probably dead, my mother took charge and found ways to keep us clothed and fed. She had me pry wood moldings from the doors and windows of abandoned houses and barter the wood for food in the market.

The Soviet military command set up their offices in a building on Skala's main street, and I applied for a job. The officers appreciated that I spoke some Russian, and my neat handwriting was useful to them because they had no typewriters. The war was still going on, and my job was mainly making lists of the local men of military age who could serve in the Red Army. The job didn't pay much, but it allowed me to buy food for my mother and brother.

The other secretaries in the office were Christians. No one is born hating Jews, but I will never forget the looks those girls gave me when I walked in for my first day of work. They were angry to see a Jew in their office. "What?" they said to one another. "She's still alive? What nerve, showing her face around here."

During my first day on the job, I received a message: Jan was in jail. The Russians had arrested him and charged him with being a German collaborator. I immediately went to see him and was taken to a cell no bigger than a closet with metal bars. When I arrived, Jan's sister was there getting ready to leave. She looked at me with a sneer and said to Jan, loud enough for me to hear, "She's not worth it, your little Jewess."

After she left, I passed some bread with honey to Jan through the bars of his cell. How sad and strange, I told myself, that now it is me giving food to Jan and not him to me. What if the rumors that he had killed my father were true? I dared not say anything to him. Who knew what else he might have done during the German occupation? I stayed awhile but we did not have a lot to say to each other. I promised to come to see him regularly and then left.

After a week in jail, Jan was released.

Later he showed up at Sidor's house and gave me a gift of white sandals made from heavy wool with white accents and platform soles. They were the first real pair of shoes I'd had in two years, and I wore them everywhere. One day, a woman ran after me and pinched my arm.

"I'd know those sandals anywhere!" she yelled. "They were custom-made for my mother—then she was killed!"

I hurried away from her and never asked Jan where or how he got the sandals.

CHAPTER FIFTEEN

Autumn 1944— Back to School

IN SEPTEMBER the war was still raging elsewhere in Europe, but for young people in Poland school was about to begin. Three years before, when the Germans had forbidden Jewish children to attend school, I'd had only one more year remaining of high school. A school was about to reopen in the nearby town of Czortkow (CHORT-cow), and I was determined to attend.

During the many months of hiding from people who wanted to kill us—months of starvation, sickness, and fear of being killed—it was education that had helped to keep me alive. I owed my life to my father's ability to recite passages from books he had read and to my own dreams of attending medical school. Now that I finally had the chance to finish high school, nothing could stop me from going.

My mother had friends in Czortkow who agreed

to rent me a room in exchange for sacks of grain my mother promised to bring them each month. After registering at the school, I found a job in a nearby government office. Each day after classes, I worked for the Russians as I had done in Skala, writing letters and doing office work.

Then I found out that Jan had rented a room nearby. He came to see me and explained that back in Skala the Russians were arresting Ukrainian police like him, so he had decided to move. He never asked my opinion about coming to live near me. He simply assumed we would go on as before. I was grateful for all he had done but terrified by the suspicion that he might have killed my father to save his own life.

Each day after work I walked to the marketplace to buy food for dinner. Some days I left the office and Jan would be standing there, waiting to walk me to the marketplace. Clearly he still loved me. In hiding when I was filthy with lice, fleas, and diarrhea, he had once said to me, "Even if you are on a train to Auschwitz, I will come and get you."

He had taken so many risks for me and my family. I don't think he would have done that if he didn't love me. But how could I pretend to love him when

I lived with the nagging suspicion that he was my father's murderer?

The marketplace in Czortkow bustled with people buying and selling, desperate to return to a normal routine they had not known in a long time. Merchants wore clothes so weary from years of war that they were practically colorless. Still, they were clearly energized by being back at work, stacking goods in piles and cooking street food in dented metal pans that sat on small kerosene stoves. The smell of fried *pyrogi*—a traditional Eastern European pastry filled with meat and onions—wafted across the market square. Merchants flipped the *pyrogi* with a flourish and called out, "Come! Buy here! The tastiest at the best price!"

Jan bought me food. Sometimes we stopped at a café for tea. Sometimes I scolded myself for selfishly continuing to see him, since there was no ignoring the differences between us. He was ten years older. He had barely any schooling. He was a non-Jew. And I had this persistent fear that he had killed my father, perhaps to prove to the Germans that he was a loyal policeman.

What was I still doing with him?

CHAPTER SIXTEEN

———

Journey to a New Life

I TURNED TWENTY-ONE IN SEPTEMBER 1945 and had no idea what my future would be. Images of Paris and New York still played in my head, but they seemed more like the foolish dreams of a girl who would never escape the bleak, impoverished world around her. One day, Jan and I climbed a hill on the outskirts of town and sat under a tree.

"My sister sent me a letter," he said. Jan's sister had never liked me. During the months we were hiding in Jan's barn, we always worried she would go to the authorities and turn us in.

"In the letter," Jan said, "my sister writes about a Polish fellow in Skala named Stephan, a Christian who fell in love with a Jewish girl. This Stephan wanted to leave his wife so he could live with that Jewish girl, but the Jewish girl fell in love with someone else. So Stephan hanged himself."

"Why are you telling me this horrible story?" I asked.

"My sister wrote," Jan replied, "that in Skala people who know about us are saying you will abandon me just like that Jewish girl abandoned Stephan. At the end of her letter, my sister even wrote, 'When are you going to hang yourself?'"

"She's horrible, your sister," I said, and could not shake the image in my mind of Jan hanging by a rope because of me. That night, I dreamed that I was digging up graves, searching for my father.

World War II ended in Europe in May 1945 when the Allies finally defeated the German army, but anti-Semitism did not end. Roaming bands of vigilantes—people who took the law into their own hands—were killing Jews on the streets of Skala. In May my mother told me and Arthur that the time had come for us to leave Skala and find a safer place to live. The government had given permission for the Jews of Skala to relocate to a refugee center in Upper Silesia, a liberated area of western Poland. We had no idea what conditions would be like there, but it had to be safer than Skala. "We'll just have to take our chances," my mother said.

Arthur and I helped our mother sell our household possessions, including some pots, an old wooden table and chair, two beds, and some clothing. With the money she bought fruit, flour, sugar, grains, and other supplies. She baked crackers and loaves of bread, which she then dried. Then she spent the next several days cooking and canning food for the journey ahead.

One day shortly before our departure, Sidor came to say good-bye. He gave us a homemade loaf of bread, which was a generous gift on his part. My mother wanted to thank him for all he had done for us. She looked around our little room, and all that was left of our belongings was an old zinc washtub, so she asked him to please take it. Sidor accepted the tub and left.

As soon as the door closed my mother burst into tears. She was ashamed. After all Sidor had done and all the risks he had taken to save our lives, the only thing we had to give him in thanks was a battered old tub. Her sadness was more than I could bear, and so I went outside for a walk. If we were leaving Skala, I wanted to visit a few places for one last time.

I walked down the main street. The houses were deserted. The wooden doors and windows were gone, stripped away for firewood. My old Hebrew school was now just an abandoned building. The library where I had spent so many hours reading was empty. All the books had been taken long ago. I had to get away, and there was only one other place I cared to visit.

It took me about an hour to reach the Turkish Tower. Not much was left of it. Most of it had fallen into heaps of stones over the centuries. I climbed one of the Tower walls and sat looking out over Skala, which seemed to me like a ghost town. Houses on the main avenue were wrecked and deserted, and despite the warm spring weather, the air blew cold. I pulled my jacket tighter around me and asked myself the question that every man, woman, and child who survived the Nazis would ask every day of their lives: Why me? Why had I been spared?

I might never know the answer to that nagging question, but the time had come to appreciate life and start living again. I had to say good-bye to Skala—to my past—and that meant also saying good-bye to Jan. Not only did I have my suspicions about his role in my father's death but also Jan was Christian. If we got married and had a child, Jan would want to put a crucifix around our child's neck. I could not live with that. Long ago, I had promised my father that my children would be practicing Jews. I could never betray that promise.

I climbed down from the Tower wall and headed back to Skala. When I got to Jan's house, he took one look at the stern expression on my face and knew why I had come. He rushed up and kissed me and held me close. From an inside jacket pocket he pulled out a folded velvet cloth and put it in my hand. I opened it, and there was a gold ring. It was his good-bye gift to me. Was it stolen? Had he removed it from the hand of a dead person? He didn't say where he had gotten the ring. He simply handed it to me, then I turned and walked out the door.

We never saw each other again.

CHAPTER SEVENTEEN

Marriage

THE TRAIN TO UPPER SILESIA took four weeks to reach its destination. During that time, my brother and I had enough to eat, thanks to my mother's forethought in preparing so much canned food. Skala—the place where we all had been born—was already fading into memory. Most of our friends and family were dead, and whatever we once possessed of value, such as silk dresses, silver candlesticks, and precious books, had been stolen long ago. Everything we owned now fit into three small bags.

In August 1945, we arrived in the town of Bytom, and for the next five months we lived in a Jewish refugee center in the middle of the town. Conditions were worse than we had imagined. Bytom was a coal-mining town, and every house was coated with a thick layer of coal dust. Even grass in the parks was black with soot. The refugee center consisted of wooden barracks with large dormitory halls. People lay on cots, exhausted, undernourished, sick, and hopeless.

Bytom was also a poor town. There was little for sale in any of the shops, and food was scarce. Once a week I stood in line at the offices of the Joint Distribution Committee (JDC), a Jewish relief organization based in New York City, waiting to receive packages of food. The JDC was an emergency relief agency that brought canned goods, medicine, and clothing to thousands of Jews who, like me and my family, had been left homeless after the war. From each weekly parcel I kept whatever my mother, brother, and I needed for ourselves. Then I bartered the rest. If there was extra flour, I traded it for meat or bread.

Our priority was to find a place to live, because anything would be better than the crowded, filthy refugee center. In the Bytom market I met an old woman who introduced herself as Miss Klampt. She would rent us a room in her apartment, she said, in exchange for us giving her an occasional bag of flour, which we received as part of our JDC packages. I accepted her offer and brought my mother and brother to her building. Our room was part of Miss

Klampt's fourth-floor walk-up apartment. The apartment had no electricity and there was only one toilet in the hall for all the tenants. Her place was sad and gray, but it was better than the refugee center.

One day a man showed up at our door and said his name was Israel. My mother recognized him as an old friend from our prewar days in Skala and explained to me that he was a matchmaker. The man looked me up and down, then said, "Out of affection for your parents, I'm going to do you a favor."

"What favor?" I asked.

"Send you a nice man to marry," he said.

Matchmaking was a legitimate occupation in those days, and the idea of my getting married made sense from a practical point of view. Our life in Bytom was miserable, and we had nowhere else to go. Maybe a good husband would be the answer to our problems.

The matchmaker sent three candidates on three separate days. My mother had me dress up in my one good white dress for each meeting. The first candidate took me to the movies. The second one took me for a walk. The third one took me for tea. All three proposed.

The candidate who took me to the movies was a sweet, gentle man named Joseph. He was blond and slim, a year older than me, and a religious Jew. He prayed every morning, ate only kosher food, and observed Shabbat. Like me and my family, Joseph had lived in hiding for two years.

He came from a shtetl, a small village near Skala. His mother had died when he was eight years old. His father was a wheat merchant and the descendent of a famous rabbi, Yom Tov Lipmann Heller. Joseph said that years ago his father had emigrated to British-controlled Mandate Palestine, the place that one day would be known as Israel. Joseph was the youngest of his six siblings and the only one still alive.

The matchmaker had told Joseph that I was a nice girl, that I was well educated, and that I came from a fine family. But he felt obliged to also tell Joseph that I had once had a non-Jewish boyfriend named Jan. It didn't surprise me that he revealed that detail of my life. He would not have done a good job as matchmaker if he neglected to tell Joseph that he was not the first man I had ever dated. Joseph was a gentleman and never mentioned it. Two days after we met, Joseph proposed to me. He promised to provide well for me and to take care of my mother and brother. I accepted his proposal.

Joseph and I were married in January 1946. With no money and no home, we wandered from one city to another. First we traveled to Budapest, Hungary, but left because we were afraid to live under the Russians, who were in charge there. We went to Paris, the city of my dreams, but it was impossible for Joseph to find work, and there were no guarantees that we would be allowed to stay. So we traveled on.

Next we took a train to Munich, Germany, and then Vienna, Austria. During the war, many of Vienna's residents had collaborated with the Nazis to hunt down Jews. Joseph and I always felt afraid being in such places. A knock on the door, a barking dog, a policeman in uniform—it didn't take much to trigger memories of a time when we had to run and hide to save our lives. We could never be comfortable living with such associations.

So we traveled on again, this time to visit Joseph's father in Palestine. We had always wanted to go to Palestine, the biblical promised land of the Jews, but the British had severely restricted how many Jews could live there. The British had Arab partners in the region and could not risk alienating them by allowing too many Jews to settle in Palestine. Those Jews who did manage to set up homes in Palestine found themselves the target of attacks by Arab nationalists.

"Things are not good here now," Joseph's father told us. "Go to America."

America, too, had strict immigration laws and restrictions, so we were obliged to return to Munich. Our first child was born there in 1946, a daughter, whom we named Miriam, after my grandmother. I was still severely underweight and emotionally traumatized by what the Nazis had put me and my family through, and I refused to let the German nurses care for my baby. The idea of turning my child over to a German was unbearable because it evoked images from my past of infants snatched from their mothers' arms and killed.

Joseph took his new family responsibilities seriously and gave his full attention to earning money. He had no formal education, but ever since childhood he had an instinct for doing business. At age nine, he had had the idea of buying old squares of chocolate, washing them clean, and reselling them as new. As an adult he could instantly recognize quality merchandise and soon became an expert in German porcelain. Together, he and I bought and sold antiques and saved the money we would need for emigrating to America.

To purchase quality porcelain we traveled to Berlin, where our second child, a son named Benjamin, after my father, was born in 1957. Two years later, we had saved enough money from buying and selling porcelain, and we prepared to sail to New York.

By that time, my mother and brother had been living in New York for nearly six years, thanks to sponsorship by David, my maternal grandmother's brother. David had left Vienna in 1938 and settled in New York, where he sold women's blouses out of a tiny shop. For years, great-uncle David met with immigration officials, and he at last succeeded in getting the papers needed for my family to emigrate from Europe. Visas for my mother and Arthur came through first, and they sailed for New York in 1951.

Eight years later, in 1959, visas were finally approved for me, Joseph, and our two children. We boarded a boat and set sail for America.

CHAPTER EIGHTEEN

―――

America

COMING TO NEW YORK was like landing on another planet. I was thirty-six years old, and everything about this bustling city amazed me. The buildings were taller, the traffic louder, the lights brighter than anything I had ever seen. As a girl in Skala I had read books about New York, but I never expected to live there and had no idea what it would be like.

I had never even met an American before arriving in New York. The feeling was exciting, magical, and scary at the same time. We were nobodies, we knew no one, and I hardly spoke English. I had no friends, no one to talk to, and even people I met who did speak Polish or German like me all told me to forget the past. Nobody wanted to hear about the Holocaust.

We now had a third child, Jacqueline, named after Joseph's father, Chaim, and it was important for me to begin pulling my share of responsibilities. I started by teaching myself English. I read English-language books and newspapers—even the dictionary. I enrolled in art history courses at Columbia University, and later I received a master's degree in psychology at the New School for Social Research.

By age forty, I was doing the bookkeeping for Joseph's growing porcelain business, and our life was gradually becoming comfortable. Still, dark memories filled my head: memories of hiding, the mystery of my father's death, and the nagging question of how such evil as the Holocaust could have occurred.

It took many years of research before the world fully understood what had happened during World War II. When the statistics were compiled, the extent of the horror was beyond imagining. We know now, looking back more than a half century later, that many millions of people, including more than six million Jews, were murdered between 1933, when Hitler was appointed chancellor of Germany, and 1945, when the war ended.

Hitler's plan had been to destroy every Jew in Europe. These victims were not soldiers killed in battle. They were civilians, including women, children, and the aged. They were murdered not because they had done something wrong but because they were Jews. Hitler hated Jews, so he killed them. Scholars studying his plans say he would not have stopped with the Jews in Europe. Had Hitler won the war, he would have tried to murder every Jew in the entire world.

For those of us who survived the Holocaust— whether in Western Europe or in Eastern Europe, where I grew up—the memory of those horrible times will never go away. We were hunted down, forced to live in tiny spaces, subjected to starvation and disease, and compelled to steal and lie just to stay alive. The result was that many survivors, including me, came away after the war thinking poorly of ourselves.

After coming to New York I started seeing psychiatrists, hoping to feel better about myself. I had my first session with a therapist in 1969, and it took two years before I could even begin to talk about what I had witnessed as a girl during the war. Most therapists in those days had no idea what to do with Holocaust survivors like me. There had never been a Holocaust before, and we survivors suffered from things doctors and therapists just didn't understand.

Still, I had to try getting out of my depression. I signed up for different kinds of therapies: Freudian analysis, Jungian analysis, scream therapy, dream therapy—ten years of therapy in an effort to feel better about myself. I started with one session a week, then three per week.

All those years of talking about what I went through helped, but what aided me even more was art. Reading classic literature, listening to great music, and looking at beautiful paintings made me feel better about myself. Art nourished my soul and gave me a reason to live. If I was sad or depressed, I went to a museum or read for an hour, and I usually felt better. Writers, composers, and painters expressed life's most difficult questions in ways that allowed me to think about those questions, too.

Does God exist? Why did the Holocaust happen? Art helped me explore such profound questions better than I ever could have done on my own. Art was my salvation. Art gave me a reason to go on living. Gradually, through a combination of therapy and art, my faith in God returned.

Something else restored my faith in God—my children. Giving birth and watching my children grow also helped me to believe again. Nothing can compare with seeing your own children become adults and have children of their own. Now, at this late stage of my life, I have twenty great-grandchildren. Amazing! They give me such joy. With so much worth living for, there could be no other conclusion for me than to again have faith in God.

As for that nagging question—why was I spared?— I have decided not to ask it anymore. I no longer question my good fortune. Call it karma or fate that I survived, or say simply, "It was meant to be." However it happened, I was lucky enough to build a good life and fill it with the things I love: family, music, art, and my beloved books.

If there was anything that could express my appreciation for such a good life in my later years, it would be telling my story to others. Personal testimony gives a human face to those who perished in the Holocaust, as well as to the survivors and their rescuers. That is why I wrote this book: so that young people could know about some of the good people in the world and what they did. When I am no longer around to talk about them in person, this book will do that for me. Now let me tell you what happened to some of the important people in my life.

My dear husband, Joseph, did well as a collector and dealer in antiques. At the end of his life, he left me with enough money to live comfortably and to support causes I believe in. For example, Joseph's money has gone to support the Museum of Jewish Heritage in New York and helped build a hospital for wounded soldiers in Israel. Joseph died in 1986 at age 63. He lived long enough to see our grandchildren reach their teen years.

My brother, Arthur, and I speak every day. He lives near me in New York City. While he never fully recovered from the trauma of his experiences as a young boy, we spend time together and love each other very much.

Our rescuer, Sidor: After settling in New York in 1960, I made many attempts to contact him. All that I could find out was that the Russians had sent him to the Soviet Union sometime in the 1950s. For many years I had no information about him at all. Yet I could never forget him. What an example he was of courage and compassion. Despite the danger to himself and his family, he hid us in his home and shared the little bit of food they had so we could survive. More than anyone, he renewed my belief in the human capacity for kindness and decency even at great personal risk.

Sidor's daughter, Hania, and I were reunited in 1995. It happened because the Soviet Union fell in 1991, and for the first time since the war we had been able to obtain information about people from home. I learned that Hania was still living in Skala, was married, and had two children. I wrote to her immediately and told her that I wanted to see her again, but I had no desire to return to Skala. There were too many painful memories there. So for a meeting place I recommended Yad Vashem, the Holocaust memorial and museum in Jerusalem. Hania agreed to meet there, and a date was set for our reunion.

In preparation for that exciting event, I applied to have Sidor accepted by Yad Vashem as one of the Righteous Among the Nations. At the time there were 19,000 people who had been honored by the museum for risking their lives to save Jews during the Holocaust without ever asking for payment.

A few months later, I received news from Yad Vashem that my request had been approved. Sidor would be accepted as one of the Righteous Among the Nations.

In 1997, Hania and her son, Boris, flew from Kiev to Israel for our reunion. I was waiting at Yad Vashem, surrounded by family and reporters with cameras. When Hania came through the door, I burst into tears. She was no longer the eight-year-old girl I had known when my family was in hiding in her father's house. Now she was in her early sixties. She still had blond hair and those beautiful dark eyes that I remembered from childhood. We held each other and pressed our foreheads together, and tears streamed down our cheeks.

I asked her what memories she had from those days. She replied that she could still remember being afraid when the Germans and their Ukrainian collaborators came looking for us. She remembered being hungry. She remembered her mother yelling at Sidor for hiding us in their home.

And she remembered what happened to Jan.

CHAPTER NINETEEN

An Unsolved Mystery

ACCORDING TO HANIA, after the end of the war Jan married the girl he had been dating when he and I broke up, and they had a daughter. It did not bother me to learn that. I cared for him and hoped he had found happiness. Sometime later, Hania said, the Russians arrested Jan and sent him to a gulag, a forced labor camp in Siberia, which was a remote, cold, and desolate part of the Soviet Union.

"What was his crime?" I asked. Hania wasn't sure.

"Maybe somebody told the Russians he had collaborated with the Nazis," she said, "or that he had been a Ukrainian partisan. We'll never know for sure." In those days, authorities rarely bothered to check if people were truly guilty of something before punishing them.

Jan remained imprisoned in that Siberian gulag for ten years. When he returned to Skala, his body was broken. He hobbled and had to use a cane when he walked. He built a home for himself, but soon he was again accused of committing a crime. This time someone said he had stolen money from Jews, and when the Russian police came they found a small amount of gold under the floorboards of his house. That was sufficient proof of guilt as far as they were concerned.

"Pack your bags," the police told Jan. "We will be back to get you tomorrow."

When the police returned the following day, Hania said, Jan was dead. He had hanged himself from a rafter of his new home.

When I think of Jan it is with great appreciation for everything he did for me and my family. I don't know if he killed my father. What I do know is that my father told him, "I like you, but my daughter will go to school after the war and can't be with you."

Jan must have been angry about that. Then there was the pressure during the war to be a good police officer, and maybe he had to prove it by killing my father. Or maybe he was angry that his family hated him for hiding us and wanted revenge. Maybe he could not tolerate the other officers calling him a "Jewish uncle" and decided to do something about it.

I will never know, and I no longer think about it. After marrying Joseph, I wanted the past to stay in the past, and I did not think about Jan. I committed myself to being a good Jewish wife for Joseph. All I wanted after liberation was to be a normal human being again and dedicate myself to doing good. I have a big appetite for that, for doing good. That's what it means to be human: to take care of each other from cradle to grave. And that became my mission in life. To help others.

CHAPTER TWENTY

Closing Thoughts

JEWS WHO SURVIVED THE HOLOCAUST live every minute with the past. I am amazed that we are still alive after so much hatred against us throughout history. I identify deeply with the Jewish people, with their resilience, with their love of learning and of family. I'm proud of being a Jew, but there is no recovering from the past. I have scars.

When I was a young mother, for example, I used to overfeed my children when they were little. I gave them juice, bananas, mini-steaks, everything I could buy, because my memories were of times when you never knew when you would eat again. My children were so full, they used to give some of the food to our dog.

At first, I wrote about my early life experiences for my children and grandchildren. I wanted them to know where they come from and what their history is. Then I began to think there are important issues to be discussed with others, not just my own family. With the survivor population advancing in age, I realized how important it was to convey our memories, especially to young people, gentile and Jew, privileged and needy.

Teachers began inviting me to speak to their students—and students asked me good questions. "Where was God?" they ask. I ask them in reply, "Where was man? Don't blame God for what people do."

A teacher at a school in Brooklyn had me back four times to speak with her students. At first, she said she wasn't sure how the students would respond to an old lady who speaks with an accent. It turned out the students were respectful, paid attention, and asked great questions. Many of her students had their own experiences of hunger or emotional suffering, and they related to my pain. I told them, "I bring you a message of hope and love. If I lived through what I went through, you can live through what you're going through." Many of them stayed after the talk to shake my hand or give me a hug and thank me. So this book is for them, too.

And it is for you, dear reader, so that you, too, can know about the past, appreciate the life you have now, and make your own contributions to a better future for all.

QUESTIONS FOR DISCUSSION

- While Fanya and her family were in hiding, Fanya's father kept everyone mentally stimulated by reciting literature and poems. How might literature help someone to survive?

- How might learning about the Holocaust from the testimony of a survivor—a witness to the tragedy such as Fanya—help you relate personally to his or her experiences?

- Fanya writes that "words such as 'moral' and 'ethical' took on different meanings" during the Holocaust. Discuss what she means by this statement.

- Only a few people in Skala were willing to help save Jews during the war. What does this suggest about the ways we judge an entire group of people?

- *Überleben* is a German word for persevering
  despite impossible odds. Death may have seemed
  inevitable, yet something compelled Fanya, her
  father, and others to demonstrate *überleben*, to
  sincerely believe they would survive and outlast
  their Nazi oppressors. What might have been the
  source of such willingness to persevere? What
  forms of resistance are mentioned in this book?
  Explain why Fanya found the partisans to be such
  an inspiration.

- Sidor's family and Fanya's family celebrated
  Christmas together. Why was this significant?

- Why did Fanya's mother feel ashamed to be able
  to give Sidor only the zinc washtub? Why was it
  important to her to give him something?

- Think back to earlier in the book, when Fanya
  described what she wanted to do with her life. Did
  she ultimately achieve her dreams?

- It is a tradition in Ashkenazi (Eastern and Central
  European) Jewish culture to name children after
  relatives who are no longer living. Fanya names

her son, Benjamin, after her father. Why do you think this is an important custom? How does naming a child after someone honor them? Do you know the history behind your name? Do you know why it was chosen for you?

- Why does Fanya continue to talk about her experiences, even though it may be painful to do so?

GLOSSARY

Aktion (plural: *Aktionen*): A brutal roundup in which the Nazis arrested and deported men, women, and children to be shot at killing sites or deported to death camps.

Anti-Semitism: Hatred or persecution of Jews. Jews have faced hatred since pre-Christian times, but it reached a climax during the Holocaust.

Belzec: One of six killing centers, or death camps, set up in German-occupied Poland primarily for the mass murder of Jews, as well as Gypsies (a slang term for the Roma and Sinti peoples) and other "undesirables." Belzec was so effective in murdering Jews that only two people are known to have survived out of a half million Jews sent there during the ten months Belzec was operating.

Collaborator: A person who willingly cooperates with an enemy force. There were people in most occupied countries who collaborated with the Nazis.

Concentration camp: A facility built by the Nazis for people they considered enemies. Many camps existed to make Jews and other "enemies" perform brutally hard labor. The Nazis built thousands of such camps.

Deportation: Removing someone from his or her home. During the Holocaust, this word began to mean forced transfer of Jews to ghettos and killing centers, usually in overcrowded, filthy trains (cattle cars) without windows, food, water, or toilets. Many people died during deportation.

Forced labor: Unpaid, physically painful work imposed on Jews and other minorities. The Nazi government drafted most German men into the army, which caused a shortage of workers. To continue production of materials for war, repairs on roads, and construction of housing, the Nazis forced men, women, and children to perform these tasks.

Gulag: Any of a network of forced labor camps in the former Soviet Union. Gulag camps existed throughout the Soviet Union, but the largest camps lay in the most extreme geographical and climatic regions of the country, from the Arctic north to the Siberian east and the Central

Asian south. The combination of violent punishment by guards, extreme climate, hard labor, meager food rations, and unsanitary conditions led to extremely high death rates in the gulag camps.

Holocaust: A word of Greek origin meaning complete destruction, especially by fire. The word is used to describe the murder of European Jewry by the Nazis and their collaborators. The Hebrew word for Holocaust is the biblical term Shoah (pronounced SHOW-ah), meaning catastrophe, destruction, or disaster.

Kosher: Literally meaning "fit" or "proper," the term applies to anything that is suitable for use according to Jewish law. Most often the word "kosher" refers to food that is acceptable by the Jewish dietary laws (kashruth). According to these laws, certain kinds of meat may not be eaten, kosher meat must be ritually slaughtered in a specified manner, and milk and meat may not be eaten together.

Mandate Palestine: An area in the Middle East that was controlled by the British from 1917 to 1947. In October 1947, the United Nations divided Palestine into a Jewish state and an Arab state. The State of Israel was officially established in 1948.

Partisan: A member of an organized fighting group that attacks the enemy within occupied territory. During World War II, partisans killed Nazis and sabotaged their war efforts. Some Jews formed their own partisan groups or family camps, while others joined existing partisan units.

Propaganda: Lies and exaggerations created to sway public opinion and spread false information.

Rescuers: "The Righteous Among the Nations," as they have been called by Yad Vashem, Israel's official Holocaust museum and memorial. Rescuers were non-Jews who provided Jews with food, hiding places, medical care, or help escaping from the Nazis. Some rescuers hid Jews in their own homes, putting themselves in great danger. Rescuers are remembered today for their courage and humanity.

Resistance: Jews actively defied the Nazis in many ways, both spiritually and physically. Many Jews engaged in spiritual resistance by keeping Jewish identity alive through education, religious observance, cultural activities, and community assistance. Others resisted by fighting with whatever weapons they could find.

Shabbat: The Jewish Sabbath, which begins on Friday evening and ends on Saturday night. It is a day of spiritual rest and reflection.

Testimony: Holocaust witnesses' firsthand accounts of their experiences, usually given in the form of audio or video recordings. Survivor testimonies differ from paper documents and other forms of evidence in that they convey the voice, emotion, and spontaneous memories of eyewitnesses.

Torah: The word Torah literally means "teaching" and refers to the first five books of the Hebrew Bible (Genesis, Exodus, Leviticus, Numbers, and Deuteronomy), or a scroll containing these books. A Torah scroll is handwritten on parchment and read out loud in the synagogue during prayer services.

The coauthors gratefully thank these advisors for their support and guidance.

Editorial Advisor
Amanda Lanceter
Senior Manager of Education Programs
Museum of Jewish Heritage: A Living Memorial
   to the Holocaust

Historical Advisor
Yitzchak Mais
Director (ret.), Yad Vashem Holocaust History Museum
Founding Chief Curator
Museum of Jewish Heritage: A Living Memorial
   to the Holocaust

Academic Advisor
Elizabeth Edelstein
Vice President for Education
Museum of Jewish Heritage: A Living Memorial
   to the Holocaust

Project Advisor
Michael Berenbaum
Professor of Jewish Studies and Director
Sigi Ziering Institute, American Jewish University,
   Los Angeles
Former President, Survivors of the Shoah Visual History
   Foundation (now the USC Shoah Foundation)

Learn more about Fanya at **www.fanyaheller.com**